WELCOME TO THE CONSTRUCTION SITE

1 Excavator

Samantha Bell

Published in the United States of America
by Cherry Lake Publishing
Ann Arbor, Michigan
www.cherrylakepublishing.com

Content Adviser: Louis Teel, Professor of Heavy Equipment Operating,
Central Arizona College
Reading Adviser: Cecilia Minden, PhD, Literacy expert and children's author

Photo Credits: ©fuyu liu / Shutterstock, cover, 2; ©Zhao jian kang /
Shutterstock, 4; ©Digital Vision. / Thinkstock, 6; ©vkp-australia /
Thinkstock, 8; ©Ralf Geithe / Shutterstock, 10; ©tverkhovinets /
Thinkstock, 12; ©Comaniciu Dan / Shutterstock, 14; ©JANIFEST /
Thinkstock, 16; ©Freestocker / Thinkstock, 18; ©Tsuguliev / Thinkstock, 20

Library of Congress Cataloging-in-Publication Data
Names: Bell, Samantha, author.
Title: Excavator / by Samantha Bell.
Description: Ann Arbor : Cherry Lake Publishing, 2019. | Includes
  bibliographical references and index. | Audience: Grades K to 3.
Identifiers: LCCN 2018003278| ISBN 9781534129177 (hardcover) |
  ISBN 9781534132375 (pbk.) | ISBN 9781534130876 (pdf) |
  ISBN 9781534134072 (hosted ebook)
Subjects: LCSH: Excavation—Juvenile literature. | Excavating
  machinery—Juvenile literature.
Classification: LCC TA732 .B45 2019 | DDC 621.8/65—dc23
LC record available at https://lccn.loc.gov/2018003278

Cherry Lake Publishing would like to acknowledge the work of The Partnership
for 21st Century Learning. Please visit *www.p21.org* for more information.

Printed in the United States of America
Corporate Graphics

Table of Contents

Why does the boom bend like an arm?

Digging and Loading

An **excavator** looks like a huge shovel on a machine. It has a large bucket. It has a long **boom**. It can do many different jobs.

It can dig large holes. It digs out basements for homes. It digs **trenches** for pipes.

It loads the dirt into dump trucks.

It loads the dirt into dump trucks.

Super Strength

Excavators can lift heavy things. They lift heavy pipes. They lift huge rocks.

They can knock down buildings.
They can cut and break buildings.

What kinds of responsibilities does an operator have?

In Control

The **operator** sits in the excavator. This area is called a cab. The cab can turn in a circle.

The operator turns the cab around. The operator can see everything at the **site**.

Getting Around

Some excavators move on wheels. Some move on **tracks**.

Excavators are powerful machines!

Find Out More

Book

Perritano, John. *Construction Machines*. New York: Gareth Stevens Publishing, 2014.

Website

The Great Picture Book of Construction Equipment
www.kenkenkikki.jp/pbe/dig/dig_005.html
Find out more about excavators at this site.

Glossary

boom (BOOM) the long, arm-like part that is used to lift and move the bucket

excavator (EK-skuh-vay-tor) a machine that prepares the ground for constructing a building

operator (AH-puh-ray-tur) someone who works a machine

site (SITE) the place where something was, is, or will be built

tracks (TRAKS) the metal or rubber belts on a vehicle that make it move

trenches (TRENCH-ez) long, narrow holes in the ground

Home and School Connection

Use this list of words from the book to help your child become a better reader. Word games and writing activities can help beginning readers reinforce literacy skills.

a	down	large	see
are	dump	lift	she
at	everything	like	shovel
basements	excavator	loads	site
boom	excavators	long	sits
break	for	looks	some
bucket	has	machine	the
buildings	he	machines	they
cab	heavy	many	things
can	holes	move	tracks
circle	homes	on	trenches
cut	huge	operator	trucks
different	in	or	turns
dig	into	out	wheels
digs	it	pipes	
dirt	jobs	powerful	
do	knock	rocks	

Index

About the Author

Samantha Bell has written and illustrated over 60 books for children.
She lives in South Carolina with her family and pets.

E BELL   FLT
Bell, Samantha,
Excavator /

01/19